Money and the Happy Way of Living

This fantastic book is a concise and straightforward guide to learning the secret of financial happiness.

Mark Pringle

Published by Arczis Web Technologies, Inc.

Money and the Happy Way of Living
Copyright © 2020 by Arczis Web Technologies, Inc.

All rights reserved. Printed in the United States of America. No part of this book may be used or reproduced in any manner whatsoever without written permission except in the case of brief quotations embodied in critical articles or reviews.

For information contact:
http://www.arczis.com/
http://www.moneyandhappyliving.com/

ISBN: 9798621220747

First Edition: March 2020

CONTENTS

ABOUT THIS BOOK 5

A PERSONAL STORY - FROM DEBT TO FINANCIAL CONTENTMENT 6

DON'T BUY THINGS, DO THINGS 17

BE THERE FOR OTHERS 25

KNOW WHERE YOU ARE SPENDING YOUR MONEY (BUDGETING) 29

SIMPLE STEPS TO GETTING OUT OF DEBT 39

SAVE, SAVE, SAVE – BUT DON'T JUST PUT MONEY IN THE BANK .. 42

STEP OUT OF YOUR COMFORT ZONE (TRAVEL AND EXPERIENCES) 48

HUMILITY CONTRIBUTES TO HAPPINESS 51

AVOID CREDIT CARDS – WELL, KIND OF 54

SMART THINKING WHEN BUYING A HOME 57

SMART THINKING WHEN BUYING A CAR 63

FIND WHAT YOU LIKE TO DO AND MAKE THAT YOUR CAREER 66

MAINTAIN BALANCE IN YOUR LIFE AND WORK 70

BUY USED - GARAGE SALES AND THRIFT STORES ARE GOOD 74

COLLEGE EDUCATION AND FINANCIAL THINKING 76

TRY TO BE SELF-SUFFICIENT 80

THE EFFECTS OF PATIENCE AND UNDERSTANDING ON HAPPINESS 82

PARENTS, TEACH YOUR CHILDREN TO WORK & MORE 87

STRATEGIC THINKING AND HAPPY DECISIONS 90

TAKE A CHANCE 92

OTHER ADVICE FOR HAPPY FINANCIAL LIVING 95

THE SECRET TO FINANCIAL HAPPINESS AND HAPPY LIVING 100

DADDY - A PROSE TRIBUTE TO MY FATHER 101

About This Book

This book is a concise and straightforward guide to financial happiness and contentment, as well as a guide for cultivating a mindset that contributes to a happy life. The principles and life stories within will help you establish financial peace of mind, eliminate and avoid debt, and find general happiness in your life.

I have included many experiences from my life and how they relate to well-established and practical economic principles. Following these principles and teaching them to your children will help to maximize your family's chances of finding long-term financial happiness and a happy state of mind.

Keep in mind that the suggestions and experiences are from the perspective of a person living in the United States. The advice you can apply will vary from country to country and economy to economy. Nevertheless, no matter where you live, you will benefit from the principles and experiences in this book. Enjoy.

A Personal Story - From Debt to Financial Contentment

There's nothing special about me. I did not come from a wealthy family. I am not good looking, although my mother might say differently. I do not have a Ph.D. in Psychology nor a Business & Finance Ph.D. I've never had what I would consider a prestigious job. I am African-American. However, the advantage I did have was two educated parents who loved me and taught me many valuable things.

Childhood and My Father

As early as I can remember, my father would invite me into his home office and talk to me about saving money. I was around five or six years old, standing next to him as he showed me his savings account. He explained the best way he could to a child the value of compounding interest, being careful with money, and saving for a rainy day. I fondly remember those conversations. Unfortunately, early in my adult life, I did not listen to his counsel.

After high school, I went to college to pursue a Fine Arts degree, but I could not afford to attend the college of my choice. I ended up attending a local university, the University of Florida.

Both of my parents valued education, and my father said he would pay for college as long as I maintained a B average and if I majored in a "real degree." To him, Fine Arts was not a "real degree." So, I changed my major and began college as a Finance major. Finance and statistics were my second loves.

Now, you have to understand that my father was the type of person who would only tell you something one time, and he expected you to adhere to that command perfectly. There were no second chances, and there were no excuses.

During my first semester of college, I had too much fun partying, playing basketball, and wasting time. As a result, I ended up on academic probation. Being on probation meant that if I did not improve my grades the next semester, I would be expelled from school. When my father asked for my grades, I told him what they were. He said, "Okay, do you remember what I told you before school started?" I said, "Yes, sir." I knew what was next. My father said, "You pay for college from now on." That was all he said.

I knew my father would not change his mind, because that's who he was. I never bothered to ask him to reconsider. I understood that if he told you something one time, you were to do it. Otherwise, you suffer the consequences.

The next semester I paid for my tuition and books, and miraculously my grades skyrocketed. I graduated four and a half years later after working and paying my way through college and changing to a Fine Arts major mid-stream. Since my father was no longer paying for school, I could major in my first love, Fine Arts.

Adult Life and Accumulating Debt

Before graduating from college in 1989, I got a $20,000 loan in anticipation of starting a commercial art business after graduation. It's still amazing to me that my mother allowed me to take out a loan secured by my parent's house (my father never knew, and I do not recommend doing this). The day after graduation, I moved to a new state with no savings and $25,000 in debt. I drew caricatures at an amusement park to bridge the gap. A few months later, I married my college girlfriend, and we settled into our new location. Soon after that, I started my commercial art business.

This period was at the start of the internet age, and I used most of the loan to buy computer equipment that would become obsolete in a few years. The business started slowly, and I was not making much money. Fortunately, my wife had a job. Still, I had to work a second job as a security guard two nights a week to help pay the bills. Two nights out of every week, I did not sleep! That was rough. However, I was content with working hard and doing what I needed to grow my business over time and make it a success.

One year into the business, my wife became pregnant, and we didn't have health insurance. Now, as a teenager, I had collected comic books and amassed close to 6,000 comics at the height of my collecting. I sold most of them to help pay for college. I used the relatively few remaining comic books to help pay for the birth of my first child. The balance of the hospital bill added to our debt.

About seven months after my first child was born, we found out that our second child was on the way. We did not have savings, nor health insurance, nor was my business earning enough money to support two children. Now, I had to get a "real job," mainly because of the lack of health insurance for my growing family.

I started working as a commercial artist for a small ophthalmic marketing company about three years into our marriage, but I was not making much money since this was my first real job after graduating from college. Even though I had worked at this company for only one year, the work experience allowed me to find a better paying job with a more stable company.

We were struggling financially over the next four years but somehow managed to save enough money to put a down payment on a house using a first-time home-buyers program. We also purchased a new car about a year before we bought the house. We accumulated these things while still $20,000 plus in debt from my failed business, credit cards, a few small college loans, and hospital bills. Now, our real financial problems began.

Financial Torture - The Debt Years

We went through a few years of what I would call financial torture. We were making just enough money to pay our bills, and it always seemed, as soon as we were about to get ahead, our car or our house would need an expensive repair. I would use credit cards to pay those bills. When those cards were maxed out, I would sign up for a new credit card. This cycle continued for a couple of years.

In those days, banks were giving away credit cards like Halloween candy. These credit cards were interest-free for a while, and some banks even gave cash for signing up. I would transfer balances from one credit card to the next so that I would not have to pay interest. Occasionally, I would apply for unsecured loans to consolidate bills, but that only seemed to make things worse. Those times were horrible, and it seemed like we were in inescapable financial quicksand.

During these tough years, my father died of a massive stroke. His death caused me to reminisce about my wonderful childhood and recall the things that my father taught me about money management. Our financial situation was so discouraging that I decided in my heart to never go through this financial agony again. I sat down with my wife and said enough is enough! We promptly decided to apply the things that my father had been teaching me since my youth. Unfortunately, we now were about $45,000 in debt from my initial business loan, credit card debt, unsecured loans, and a new car loan. The car loan was only a fraction of the debt. We were in more debt than my yearly salary, and this did not include the mortgage on our house. Being under an avalanche of debt was a horrible way to live, but I only had myself to blame.

Escaping Financial Hell - How We Got Out of Debt

Fortunately, while this self-inflicted suffering was happening, I was doing quite well at my job and receiving yearly raises. We decided to put every raise, bonus, and any other unexpected money we received towards our debt. Every extra penny would go towards paying off debt, and there would be no exceptions.

We would pay off the smallest debts first and use the money that we saved from that debt to pay off the next debt. This approach proved to be a very effective way to reduce our debt as fast as possible. During these years, we did not go out to dinner, we did not go on vacations, and we did very little in the way of entertainment that cost money. It was a time of complete dedication to paying off debt and getting our financial life in order. It took us about four years to get to the point of having a substantial cushion in our monthly expenses. Even then, we did not let up and continued in our quest to pay off the remaining debt. We were in what athletes call "The Zone." It got to the point where I was excited to pay off a bill. I eagerly anticipated tackling the next item on the list. Every raise, every tax refund, every bit of extra money went to paying off debt. We became almost fanatical in our mission to see our liabilities at zero.

It took discipline and approximately six years, but we eventually paid off all of our debt, except for our house. We would have paid it off sooner, but we purchased a new home in the interim and a new minivan, which we paid off a year after we bought it.

With no debt other than our house, our living became comfortable, almost effortless, and we became much, much happier. Aside from my marriage, the birth of our two children, and one other event, this was the most significant occasion in our lives. We vowed never to go back to that previously miserable lifestyle.

Happiness and Contentment After Debt

The Bible says in Proverbs 22:7 that, "...the borrower is a slave to the lender." Well, we were no longer slaves. There's an African saying, "If you borrow a man's legs, you will go where he directs you." Our financial obligations were no longer directing us. I had a good job, money to spend, equity in my house, and savings in the bank. We were happy, content, and could do what we wanted. What we wanted was to travel. The travel bug was a strong desire, the seeds of which were planted long ago in my youth.

Traveling soon became a passion for me and my wife, and we have traveled extensively. Occasionally our friends and family asked us how we could go on vacation so much. They knew we were not independently wealthy. They knew we did not have high paying jobs. I would tell them that we lived below our means and did not have debt. That financial freedom gave us considerable latitude. Eventually, we would have even more flexibility in our life.

Our Exit Strategy and More Flexibility in Life

A Fortune 500 company employed me for about 14 years. During this time, I was a user-interface designer, but they sent me to school to learn how to program for the web. This company needed a reasonably complex intranet website and wanted me to assist in its development. I used the skills that I learned during this part of my career to start my own business on the side. I began developing websites.

Frankly, the building of websites started as a way to hone my programming skills and learn the technology better. I was not thinking of it as a business. However, one day I was looking at a website in a particular niche and thought to myself, "You can build a better site than that." Now, the website I was looking at was a leader in the industry, and it was making a considerable amount of money. I thought if I could make a fraction of what they were making, that would help pay for our vacations, since traveling was now our passion. Additionally, building a website was a low-cost endeavor. It did not require much money to start or maintain since I had or was learning all of the skills needed to do it.

After work, I would spend an hour or two learning the technology and building the website, and after a few months, it was ready to release to the public. I was so excited the first time it made a few dollars through advertising revenue. In time, it was making a few dollars a day, and we would use that money to go out to dinner. In time, the website began to make more money; $100 a month, $200, and then more. We decided to start using this extra money for vacations. In a couple of years, the income generated by this part-time endeavor began to make enough money to pay for multiple vacations and also helped increase our savings. My wife and I said we would never rely on this money for our bills. We would use it only for fun stuff. Boy, we were very wrong. The website started making so much money that I began to wonder if we could survive off the income. Remember, this was at a time in our life when we had no debt other than our mortgage. I was also making the most money I had ever made in my secular job. The income from my "hobby" brought in even more money. Even though we were making more money than we ever had, and we had no debt, we downsized into a smaller house, which reduced our mortgage to almost half the previous mortgage. Our children were now adults, and we did not need the bigger home. It was at this time that I started planning my exit strategy from my corporate job to focus more on ministry work and helping others.

Thinking about leaving the job that was such a security blanket for 14 years was nerve-wracking. Nevertheless, my wife and I decided to go for it, and I planned on leaving corporate America. In the interim, I heard rumors that our sector of the software development department was going to be laid off. Typically, this would be disturbing news. However, since I was already planning on resigning, this was good news. Why? If I had quit, I would not receive any financial compensation from the company. However, if our sector was laid off, I would receive a severance package. I didn't know how much, but something was better than nothing.

It was the end of the fiscal year, and I waited a while to see if the rumors were true. After the end of the fiscal year, I waited a week, two weeks, and then three weeks. I heard nothing. Then, week four, I received a call from my corporate headquarters in New Jersey saying that our department was being laid off. I was thrilled! I received a severance package equal to six months of my salary. I immediately began to "officially" start and focus on my web development business. Within a year of being laid off, my websites were making more money than the highest salary at my corporate job.

This newfound situation gave us even more freedom in our day-to-day life since the maintaining of websites did not require much time and effort. It was also a business that I could do from anywhere in the world as long as I had internet access. I was content.

Having the most successful business in the world was not my goal. Nor was I focused on getting rich. We had more than enough to money live on and to do some of the things that we loved to do, like travel and help others. That was enough for my wife and me, and we began to experience "the happy way of living" to a greater extent.

When you can psychologically get to a point where enough

money is enough, and you are not wealthy, that is a great place to be. We eventually sold the house we had downsized into, as well as almost everything we had accumulated in 26 years of marriage and the raising of a family. We then moved to another country to help others through our ministry work. At last, we were completely debt-free!

I wonder if we would have been able to get out of that bad financial situation if I had not been educated on fiscal responsibility at an early age by my father. I don't think we would have. Thank you, Dad, for the knowledge and discipline you instilled in me!

Don't Buy Things, Do Things

The accumulation of things has never been an attraction for me. I guess that's a result of my upbringing. My parents were never ones who accumulated things; however, they were people who liked to amass experiences. That outlook influenced me.

My mother was a soccer mom before that phrase become popular. She was a physical education teacher and had my older brother and me participating in every sport imaginable. During my childhood, I played every little-league sport offered in our area, including baseball, football, and street hockey. I was even on a track club at an early age and received a lifeguard certification at nine years old. Possessing things was never a part of my childhood, but doing things was integral.

We learned at an early age to have fun doing things that required little money. However, there were occasions when learning experiences cost money.

When I was around three or four years old, my grandparents took us to Puerto Rico. We lived in New Jersey at the time. I only have one vivid memory from that trip, since I was too young to appreciate it, but the awareness of experiencing things began to be instilled at my core. A few years later, our parents took us to Hawaii. I do remember a significant portion of that vacation, even though I was only about seven years old at the time. As a result of experiences like these in my formative years, I was more focused on doing things than accumulating things as an adult.

Also, a desire to explore the world was forming.

Don't get me wrong; I went through periods in my life where I bought things or, more accurately, collected items. For example, as a youth, I collected coins, baseball and football cards, and comic books. Now, neither of my parents were collectors, so I'm not sure where this love originated. Nevertheless, I had close to 6000 comic books during my high school years. That investment helped pay for college and the birth of my first child. This type of "buying" proved to be valuable. Generally speaking, however, experiences always trumped things in our family.

Happiness

Have you ever noticed that occasionally you see people, who by most measures, should be happy? They have excellent health. They have more than enough money. They have a good job, a beautiful house, and a wonderful core group of friends. However, these individuals always seem to be unhappy.

On the other hand, you see someone who, by most standards, should be miserable. They might have chronic health problems or had an abusive childhood. They may have financial issues, or you notice them going though severe family problems. In spite of their circumstances, they exude joy! They seem always to have a positive outlook and disposition. Happiness is their true nature.

What is the difference? Often the difference is that the inherently happy people get joy out of living itself in spite of their circumstances. These people do not look to some "thing" to make them happy. What does this mean?

As expected, most people experience a measure of happiness when they reach a specific goal or acquire a desired item. For instance, you may see a businesswoman with a big smile on her face as she receives a promotion for a well-done job. Her happiness is real. You may know a man who is thrilled by new golf clubs and the anticipation of using them. Both of these individuals are happy, but how long does this rush of happiness last? Typically, the joy is only temporary, and many people will buy more things or set more goals to fulfill that natural desire for this feeling to continue.

Understand that setting goals is a good thing to do, and there is nothing wrong with buying things you need or even occasionally want, but do you rely on these things to make you happy, or do you get your primary enjoyment out of life itself? If you examine it, the requirements for a happy life are relatively simple: good health, adequate food, loving family and friends, clothing and shelter, peace and security, and a purpose in life. For many people, some or all of these things are hard to attain, but even if you cannot achieve all of them, you can still be happy.

Learn to Enjoy Life, Family, and Good Friends

Merriam-Webster defines life as "the sequence of physical and mental experiences that make up the existence of an individual." Notice how this definition relates "experiences" to "life." We can thus conclude that a large part of enjoying life comes from accumulating experiences and not things.

It is not a mistake that humans have five senses: touch, vision, smell, hearing, and taste. It is not a mistake that humans have these senses and live on a beautiful and fascinating little blue ball called Earth, which satisfies all of these senses. Our five senses allow us to experience life in a way that facilitates happiness.

We need to learn to appreciate hearing and enjoying the voices of our friends, loved ones, and people of differing backgrounds. We need to acquire a love for nature so that we can get full use of our sight, smell, and touch. Savor the moments when you see a majestic snow-capped mountain or when you examine the intricacies of a flower's petal. On a whim, go off the beaten path and randomly explore, the same way you went through life as a carefree child running through the rain and playing fun games outdoors.

Make it an integral part of your life to engage in some physical activity. Our bodies are designed for physical activity. If we are not using our bodies for their intended purpose, then our bodies will not be happy, and it will minimize our happiness. Use your voice to laugh and to make others laugh. According to Charles Dickens, "There is nothing in the world so irresistibly contagious as laughter and good humor."

Yes, enjoying life itself costs very little money.

Fun Things to Do That Don't Cost Much

There seems to be an unwritten rule that you must spend money to have fun. That is certainly not true. Here are some fun things that you can do that cost little or no money.

- Engage your artistic/creative side: draw, write, read, cook, or make handmade crafts and gifts
- Encourage other people
- Be active: enjoy nature, go camping, and explore your region
- Learn to play a musical instrument
- Play sports
- Read
- Spend time with friends/family: have a game night, meal-making day, or movie night
- Take up bicycling
- Take up photography. Everyone has a camera phone.
- Workout
- Write a book
- Write poetry

Create your own list. Make a list of things that are truly valuable to you, and that don't require money. Determine how to increase the time and energy you dedicate to the items on your list.

Be Content Without Things

We live in a culture that promotes and glorifies buying things. We are bombarded each day with advertisements that influence us to buy things that we do not need. What is even worse is that this constant bombardment alters our thinking to make us less and less content with the necessities of life; adequate food, clothing, shelter, and upbuilding relationships. It has become so bad that some people view shopping as a form of entertainment. We must learn to be content without things. Things do not cause happiness, nor do they make us more secure.

Sure, buying clothes, electronic gadgets, and things like these can be fun. Buying things may provide a temporary feeling of happiness, but there is no lasting joy in being focused on buying things. The fact is that those who live for money and material acquisitions frequently suffer for it. They may sacrifice families, relationships, and health for material things or riches. They are doing the opposite of what causes real happiness. Real contentment and happiness can only be achieved only by placing material things in their proper place. If you are not happy without things, you will not be satisfied very long with them. Things do not give one a purpose in life, they do not secure good health, and they do not buy quality relationships.

Impulse Buying and the Tiger Woods PGA Tour Video Game

Whenever I am tempted to buy something on the spur of the

moment, I remember the Tiger Woods PGA Tour video game I purchased many years ago.

I was shopping at a local office supply store, and I saw a Tiger Woods PGA Tour video game in the clearance bin. The new version of the game was just released, and this was the previous version. It was on sale for a ridiculously low price, and I couldn't help but purchase it. Now, I was not an avid video game player, but the price was so tempting that I had to buy it. I went home and began playing it. After about 30 minutes, I stopped, put the game on my office shelf, and never played it again.

The is experience has laughingly become an impulse buying touchstone for our family. Whenever I see something and am tempted to buy it on a whim, I remember this video game, and it keeps me in check.

What I also find funny about this experience is that it was entirely out of my nature to buy anything on impulse, but the price was so tempting that I rationalized it would be irresponsible for me not to buy it. Maybe I thought it would help my golf game.

When You Do Buy, Buy Quality

When purchasing things that you need, sometimes it is good to pay more. For example, when buying a high-quality piece of furniture, there is often a more significant outlay of money. However, paying more for higher quality may prove to be less expensive over time than buying cheaper furniture you must replace several times. A bargain may not be a bargain if the lower priced item represents a sacrifice of quality.

When Buying is Good (Collecting)

The hobby of collecting can be a fun lifelong pursuit that is financially responsible. Acquiring, organizing, learning about, cataloging, and preserving something you have a great deal of interest in, and which increases in value over time, can prove to be a good investment of money and time, assuming you do not go into debt to acquire the collection.

Adults and children collect many things, including cars, comic books, dolls, coins, train sets, sneakers, books, baseball memorabilia, and just about anything you can think of. When you make it a lifelong pursuit, you can even become an expert about the thing collected, and people will pay for your expertise.

Many children who start collecting at an early age develop good careers around the things obtained. There are few things better than loving your work and making a living doing it. Collecting can also lead to strong friendships between people with similar interests.

Keep in mind that collecting is different than buying things for the high that results from buying. These impulse buyers often lose interest in the item purchased, and there are no long-term benefits. Still, it is wise to count the cost of pursuing a hobby centered around collecting. Consider both the time and the expense involved, especially when the collection is not an investment, and you are not looking to monetize it long term.

Be There for Others

We were at a point in our life where we had the flexibility and money to step out of our comfort zone and help others more. My wife's mother was still independent and living on her own. My mother, who has dementia, was being taken care of by my sister. Our children were grown and living on their own. So, my wife and I decided to use this opportunity to sell everything that we owned and move to another country to help with ministry work.

We sold the house that we had only been living in for four years and made a nice profit because of applying the house-buying principles my father taught me. We sold everything we owned except for our minivan and sentimental personal items which fit in a 5' x 5' storage space. We were entirely debt-free now because we didn't have a mortgage.

With only five suitcases in hand, we boarded a plane and moved to Europe to help others. Of course, we could have stayed in the USA and done the same, but our spirit of adventure motivated us to seek someplace different and new. Additionally, we wanted to see how we would handle being out of our language and cultural comfort zone.

The years we spent overseas were, quite frankly, the happiest and most satisfying years of our lives. We gained friends from all over the world, all while helping others to better their lives.

As a part of this ministry work, we would often drive

hundreds of miles every week visiting people and helping them build a happier life. Sometimes, we would even drive to a different country to do this. All of this was done using personal financial resources. We were not getting paid, and we never regretted using our money in this way. We became much more enriched and happier through these experiences and newfound relationships. When you see that through your assistance, others become happier, it can be one of the greatest joys you'll ever experience.

Our experience confirms a Bible proverb that says, *"There is more happiness in giving than there is in receiving."* No words have ever been more accurate.

Helping Others Leads to Happiness

Michael J. Wagner, an author and economist, seems to agree. In his book, *Your Money, Day One,* aimed at motivating youths to save, he states, "When you take it upon yourself to help those who are less fortunate, that kindness and generosity will come back to you in a variety of positive ways, but most rewarding is the feeling you will experience in your heart by helping your fellow man."

Much of the advice in the book you are reading deals with how to increase your chances of personal financial contentment and happiness. It motivates us personally and helps the improvement of our particular lot in life. However, I am not advocating selfishness. I am promoting the opposite.

When you are happy and content with your life, it is so much easier to share that happiness with others. You will want to help others, and you will get more joy in doing this than by focusing on yourself. You will also learn that the relationships you strengthen through the assisting of others become more valuable than money. Chris Farrell, in his book *The New Frugality*, says, "When you think about what matters most, it's usually relationships, experiences, and the sense of making a difference, not money and possessions."

Ways to Help Others

Being a generous giver of your time and energy leads to happiness. According to one article, "People report a significant happiness boost after doing kind deeds for others." So, be interested in the welfare of others and look for ways to help those who are within your sphere of influence. Note that sincerely generous people do not give to receive something in return, so make sure that your motives are pure. Here are some ways to help others.

- Volunteer
- Be a mentor
- Donate time, money, or items to those in need
- Perform random acts of kindness. For example, pay the bill of the person behind you in a convenience store line
- Offer to babysit
- Say yes to a neighborhood kid who wants to do yard work

- Send a meaningful and encouraging text or email
- Say something kind about that person where others can hear
- Be a listening ear, even if you cannot practically help
- Do household chores for an elderly person

There are many things we can do to help others and make them feel good. Be creative and think about what you can do.

Know Where You are Spending Your Money (Budgeting)

I called them family financial summit meetings. Usually two or three times a year, my wife and I would have a "business meeting" to review our family budget. For many, the word "budget," brings to mind unpleasant images of long ledgers with endless rows of figures, but for our family, it was a necessary step to maintaining our financial stability. We would often include our children in these meetings to help them learn the benefits of this process.

We would review, not only our budget, but how much money we were saving. We would also try to determine if there were any bills that we could eliminate. Unfortunately, we did not start having these financial summit meetings until most of our debt was gone. It certainly would have been easier and faster to get our economic life in order if we had included this process earlier.

I don't remember any particular financial meeting standing out. However, there was a time when I was paying all of our household bills. I had a stranglehold on the checkbook. During one of our meetings, my wife expressed concern over her limited control over the money. After a lengthy discussion, we decided that she would be in charge of the household finances. Giving up control was very difficult for me because I had managed our money since we got married, and this was many years later.

It wasn't that I didn't trust my wife; it was that I believed in my frugality more. Still, I turned the majority of the household finances over to her to appease her concerns. It turned out to be the right decision. She proved to be financially responsible, and it took some household responsibilities off of my plate. We have not looked back since, and I am delighted to have a wife that is on the same financial page as I am.

Our children are adults now, and we are in good financial shape, but we still have those periodic family budget meetings.

You Work Hard for Your Money; Keep It

You work very hard for your money; however, it seems like it buys less and less every day. With that in mind, it is essential to know where your money is going every month. On what things are you spending your money? The problem is that many people do not like to be confined by a budget, nor do they even want to hear the word budget. They often cringe at the idea of keeping track of what they spend. If that's the case for you, call it "financial planning" instead of "budgeting."

Humor aside, budgeting your money is one of the first steps to financial happiness. Conversely, a lack of budgeting skills often leads to overspending, debt, and increased unhappiness. When you are on a budget, you save better, and you don't buy things that you don't need.

How to Create a Budget

Creating a budget is simple. First, list all of your monthly sources of income: salary, interest from savings accounts, pay for odd jobs, and the like. Write the amount you make on average from each of those sources of revenue.

Next, write down all of the things you spend money on each month, your expenses. You can use a pencil and a sheet of paper or a computer program to document this information. Concerning expenses, most people spend money on things like rent or a mortgage, food, electricity, internet and cable TV, gas for a car, and clothes. There are other things many people spend money on, like gym memberships, coffee, manicures, alcohol or cigarettes, lottery tickets, or donations to charities. Even if the expense seems insignificant in your eyes, write it down. List everything you spend in a typical month. If you are unsure of how you spend your money, at the end of each day, write down everything you spend and how much you spent. Do this for one month. Additionally, you can view your bank statements or credit card statement to see how you are spending your money.

After you list your monthly expenses, write down your quarterly, semiannual, annual, and other periodic bills. For example, you may pay your life insurance, car taxes, or your homeowner's association fees quarterly. Divide the amount by the appropriate number of months and add that amount to the list of your monthly expenses. You may have to estimate some of these.

After listing all of these expenses, indicate how much you spend, in an average month, for each of them. Total that number. If you make more money than you spend, this is called disposable income. It is good to have your disposable income no less than 15% of your income. Many sources will say a minimum of 20% is best.

If you are a person who is already out of debt and financially responsible, no more than 50% of your income should go to expenses. Divide the other 50% between savings and enjoying life experiences.

Example Budget

According to the book *Money Management*, "Making ends meet does not involve earning more or spending less; it is simply a matter of matching income and expenditure in advance so that life can be more pleasant." This budget example will show you how to compare and document income and expenses so you can make ends meet so your life can be happier.

What to Do

1. List your monthly income
2. List your monthly expenses
3. Subtract your expenses from your income
4. List your savings
5. Talk about the results

6. Have periodic budget meetings

Income

Don't include uncertain income, such as that from overtime pay, bonuses, or gifts.

Income - Monthly	
Job	5,115.61
Hobby/Business	300.00
INCOME - TOTAL	**5,415.61**

Expenses

One thing that people often forget to add to their monthly expenses is savings. Many may not consider it an expense, but if you think of your savings as money for emergencies, then it makes sense to add it here.

One additional thing I like to indicate is the method I use to pay the bill. I may pay by bank draft (BD), credit card (CC), check (CK), and so on. For instance, I use credit cards to pay specific bills so I can accumulate points to use on fun things like a night at the movies. Only use credit cards to pay bills if you are *extremely disciplined* and pay off the credit card immediately.

Expenses - Monthly	
Mortgage	1,178.63
Health Insurance	752.00
Electric	130.00
Gas-House	95.00
Water & Sewage	60.00
Garbage	12.99
Gas-Car-1	240.00
Gas-Car-2	70.00
Cable TV & Netflix	86.99
Car Insurance	165.17
Prescriptions	30.00
Family Entertainment	160.00
Landscaping Service	143.78
Dry Cleaning	40.00
Life Insurance	22.75
Gym Membership	39.99

Coffee and Lunch	320.00
Groceries/Personal Items	520.00
HOA (Yearly/12)	30.00
Car Taxes (Yearly/12)	15.00
Hair and manicures	150.00
Savings (10%)	500.00
EXPENSES - TOTAL	**4,762.30**

Disposable Income

Disposable income is income after taxes and minus expenses.

Disposable Income	
Income	5,415.61
Expenses	-4,762.30
DISPOSABLE INCOME - TOTAL	**653.31**

Savings

Many financial advisors recommend saving at least 20% of your take-home income every month. However, 5% should be the bare minimum. As a minimum, try to accumulate enough savings to where your family can survive if you don't have income for six months.

Savings	
Bank Savings	19,028.75
IRA	10,865.92
Pension / Retirement	19,666.04
SAVINGS - TOTAL	49,560.71

Budgeting is a Family Affair

When coming up with a budget, involve all members of the family, especially young children. According to the book, Budgeting, by Denise Chamber, "All family members should be included in drawing up the plan so that all commit to the family budget." Including your young children in periodic family meetings, where you discuss how you are doing with your budget, is a great way to give them a happy financial foundation.

Uncontrolled spending leads to unhappiness, so a family should agree on what bills are unnecessary and what expenses can be eliminated from the budget. Unfortunately, money can be one of the most challenging subjects for a family to discuss calmly. Remember, arguments over money are typically not about the money itself but trust or fear. Discuss as a family any concerns you have about your financial plan.

Budget Busters - Don't Spend Money on These Things

In today's world, it seems like it is human nature to spend money on things that do not contribute to our well-being. While these things may not be harmful in themselves, it is common to spend money on these overpriced or unnecessary items.

- $5 Cups of Coffee – Do I need to say why? Five dollars?
- Bottled Water – If you live in an area that has drinkable tap water, this is a big waste of money.
- Lottery Tickets – It's better to put that money in a place where it can grow instead of fantasyland.
- Eating Out – It's fun to eat out occasionally but doing so daily or a few times a week is too much.
- Cigarettes – Not only are cigarettes costly, but they are also long-term money stealers because they increase your health costs.
- On-Demand Movies – There's a danger in point-and-click purchases because you don't realize how many movies you bought until the bill arrives
- Movie Theater Snacks – You know that $12 for popcorn and a medium soft drink is too much.
- Name Brand Prescription Drugs – Often, but not always, generic prescription drugs have the same benefits as name

brand prescription drugs and are much cheaper.
- Professional Manicures and Pedicures – This is a luxury, not a necessity. Besides, it is better to bond with a friend and do each other's manicures and pedicures.
- Premium Cable TV – There are many less expensive options, such as cutting the cord, or subscription services for only the channels you actually watch.
- Premium or Name Brand Products – Unless there's a significant difference in quality, buy off-brand.

Budgeting Keys to Success

- Establish a pattern of healthy spending
- Learn to talk about the budget calmly
- Put the budget in writing, date it, and sign it
- Review your budget monthly to see how you are doing

Diligently sticking to your budget is essential to financial happiness. Therefore, plan and consult before spending. Keep in mind that you cannot buy everything you want, and even if you could, doing so would be unwise. Knowing how to budget your money allows you to be a happy saver. We will be discussing saving in the next chapter.

Simple Steps to Getting Out of Debt

Most people in debt understand how they got there. The accumulation of debt is a way of life. Mounting financial obligation creates a strain on family relationships and leads to many other difficulties. Frankly, getting into debt is easy. Conversely, getting out of debt can be difficult, albeit the most worthwhile thing you've ever done for your health, mental well-being, and happiness.

As you read in the initial chapter of this book, getting out of massive debt can be accomplished. I did it, and you can do it too. It is not too late for you, even if you feel that you are under a mountain of bills and other financial commitments.

If you found yourself under a landslide of dirt or snow, how would you proceed to get out? No doubt, you would start digging a little at a time. That is the same principle for getting out of a landslide of financial obligations. Here's how you should start digging.

1. Make a mental commitment to eliminate all of your debt.
2. Stop acquiring new debt and using credit cards.
3. Communicate with your family your expectations and get them to buy into your debt elimination goals. Discuss how everyone can reduce expenses or increase the family's income.

4. Reduce your expenses. See what expenses you can immediately eliminate like cable TV, landscaping services, gym memberships, or other non-essential expenses.
5. Determine your current budget.
6. Now, start paying off the smallest debt first and then use the money from that bill to pay off the next obligation. If your debts are similar in amount, pay off the higher interest rate debts first. Do not consolidate bills or get a home equity loan.
7. When you receive a raise, tax refund, or other unexpected money, use that to pay off a debt.
8. As you begin making progress, do not slow down. Have family meetings to discuss your progress. Help your family to be determined to pay off all debt.
9. When your progress is substantial, start saving 15% of your disposable income.

Other Things to Consider

Most likely, you are already working a full-time job. However, if you can find ways to increase your income, do so. Be leery about taking on a second job since that may negatively affect family dynamics and relationships, which should still be a priority while you are paying down debt.

If you find that there is absolutely no way for you to make all of your payments on time, talk to your creditors, and attempt to renegotiate the terms of the loans. For instance, some credit card companies, or other creditors may be willing to decrease your interest rate. Persist in asking if you are initially denied.

Not All Debt is Bad

All debt is not bad. Sometimes, borrowing money to help you finance an investment, can be a good decision. For example, a house is an investment, and people typically borrow money to buy their home. This type of debt can be considered reasonable since a good home increases in value over time.

Save, Save, Save – But Don't Just Put Money in the Bank

As I mentioned in my introductory story, my father would periodically invite me into his home office to explain the value of saving. I can still remember standing next to him as a child and looking at my savings ledger and his. I was not putting money into the bank as a seven-year-old, though that would have been a good thing to do, but my father was putting the money in my account to teach me. I never saw any of that money because of tax problems my father had in later years but having this explained to me as a child was the coolest thing. Even then, I could appreciate the value of saving and compounding interest thanks to my father and I have passed that understanding down to my own children.

For example, I encouraged my son to open a savings account by telling him that every time he put money in savings, I would match the amount. As a child, my son would trek throughout the neighborhood, cutting grass for our neighbors. He would put most of that money into savings, and I would match it. When he became a teenager, he was making so much money that I could no longer match his deposits. I smiled, and I told him I would only match a percentage.

Saving for a Rainy Day

The adage "save for a rainy day" suggests that every figurative day will not be happy, bright, and full of joy. We will have days of gloom and unexpected trauma, and we must assume that bad times will come. So, you must have cash in the bank to help protect yourself from those times. A Bible proverb says, "For wisdom is a protection just as money is a protection, but the advantage of knowledge is this: Wisdom preserves the life of its owner." Money cannot protect you if you don't have it, and it is the course of wisdom to save it.

According to debt.org, "Most cases of bankruptcy aren't caused by reckless spending but by financial hardship." This suggests that people did not expect nor anticipate difficult times. Not only should we plan for difficult times by saving money, but we should expect difficult times.

Ways to Save Cash

- Get a large jar and put all of your change in it at the end of each day.
- Have a portion of your paycheck deposited directly into your savings account so that you never see the money. You don't miss what you don't see.
- Pay off credit cards quickly. If you pay off a credit card that is charging you 12% a month, you have saved 12%.
- Participate in company stock purchase programs.
- Participate in company savings match plans. If someone

wants to give you money to save, do it!

Compounding Interest

Compounding interest is simply the interest you earn from the interest you've already earned. It is interest on interest. When you put your money in an account that makes interest, the money earned by the accumulation of that interest can be astonishing. In fact, in times past, the interest earned in about ten years exceeded the original amount of money invested. Imagine putting $10,000 in an account that earns interest and earning $10,000 more without ever adding more money. The current economy may not allow extreme growth like that to happen, but it does show the value of compounding interest.

Cost Cutting is Saving

Saving money not only involves regularly putting portions of your paycheck into a savings account, but it also includes adding cost-cutting measures into your daily life. Here are some simple things you can do to save money. While some of these suggestions may not apply where you live, consider the principle behind the advice and figure out when and how to use it in your life.

- Avoid greed. Remember that happy living is more beneficial than striving after lots of money.
- Don't live in a high cost of living area if you can avoid it. Look at the taxes of the county in which you live. Moving 5 miles to another county may save you hundreds of

dollars a year.
- Turn off lights, computers, appliances, and TV's when not using them.
- Get multiple quotes when having expensive work done
- Learn to do your home repairs. A $15 home improvement book can save you thousands of dollars over time when you use it to learn to do your home repairs.
- Use public transportation, carpool, walk, or ride a bike to places you might otherwise drive. My family doctor would ride his bike to work every day. As a result, he saved money, and his health improved, which saved him even more money.
- Find alternatives to cable tv that might be less expensive. Many less-expensive online services allow you to watch episodes of shows after they have aired.
- Use smaller wattage light bulbs. I did this and saved about $300 in one year.
- Close windows and use drapes in the summer to keep your house comfortable. We did this while living in Portugal. It allowed us not to use our air conditioning one summer, and we saved about $120 a month that summer.
- Turn the thermostat down in the winter
- Cancel memberships you don't use. You know, that gym membership you use once a month.
- Hang your clothes outside to dry. Yeah, I know. There is a

certain stigma attached to doing this in some areas. However, if you live in a rural area, or you have a big yard, you may be able to do it without the neighbors complaining and save money on electricity.
- Avoid wasting food. Eat leftovers. Buying groceries often takes the most considerable bite out of the family budget. Being frugal here can save money.
- Eat out less. It is usually less expensive to buy ingredients and cook meals at home than it is to eat out.
- Never be preoccupied with getting rich. People who do often put themselves in dire financial situations. A Bible proverb says, "...those who are determined to be rich fall into temptation and a snare and many senseless and harmful desires that plunge men into destruction and ruin." An overwhelming desire to get rich will more often than not lead to financial ruin.
- Grow your own fruit and vegetables.

Transportation

- Buy well-maintained used cars.
- Buy liability insurance only if your used car's value is less than $5000, and you have enough savings to self-insure.
- Keep your vehicle serviced and well-maintained as specified by the manufacturer.
- Buy a used car that gets excellent fuel efficiency (gas mileage).

- Change the oil regularly in your car and maintain proper tire pressure.

When Buying Things

- Compare prices from store to store.
- Make use of coupons and rebates.
- Borrow movies and books from the library instead of buying them.
- Purchase energy-efficient appliances.
- Purchase needed items on sale and offseason.
- Buy items/clothes from discount or secondhand stores

Maintaining is Saving

The person who saves and cuts costs grows in appreciation of the value of things. By maintaining your home, appliances, and your cars to avoid more significant expenses and you will save even more.

Once a year, my father would initiate spring cleaning. I would have to wax the floor in my bedroom. I hated doing that, but it showed me the value of maintaining things.

When your things are well-maintained, you will get more joy and satisfaction out of them.

Step Out of Your Comfort Zone (Travel and Experiences)

A few years ago, we decided to sell our home, all of our belongings, and go on a ministry trip to help others in another country. We were in a good financial situation after applying all the principles in this book, and we had the flexibility to do so.

We decided to sell everything we had accumulated over 27 years of marriage and the raising of two children. Getting rid of this stuff was not difficult because we never really developed an attachment to things. Of course, we kept a few sentimental items, but the rest of our belongings were easy to sell. The possessions we kept fit in a 5'x5' storage unit. That was the sum of 27 years of our lives.

We moved to a different country where the people spoke a different language, and it was the best experience of our lives. Stepping out of our comfort zone helped us to become more humble people. When you live in a country where you do not speak the language, it almost forces humility on you, and that's a good quality in a person. It helps you to be more tolerant of people in similar situations in your own country. Additionally, we learned more about history, human nature, and people through this experience and other travels than we ever learned in school. Our growth was a blessing.

What We Learn by Experiencing

I am a firm believer that the more cultures we experience, and the more we step out of our comfort zone, the more well-rounded, understanding, tolerant, and happy we become. Studies support this view.

Thomas Gilovich, a psychology professor at Cornell University, made four studies on the subject of happiness and concluded that happiness is obtained through experiences and not things. He went on to say, "People often think spending money on an experience is not as wise an investment as spending it on a material possession…They think the experience will come and go in a flash, and they'll be left with little compared to owning an item. But in reality, we remember experiences long afterward…"

I don't know how much we've spent on traveling over the years, but it's probably close to $70,000. In spite of this excessive amount of money, my wife and I have never once regretted spending money on these travel experiences. However, I have frequently regretted spending money on things. I have relived my travels over-and-over again, and it makes me happy doing so. I will often even write about our trips to impress them indelibly upon my mind. Even the anticipation of our next travel adventure brings me happiness.

Of course, this happiness and personal development are

dependent upon having the correct attitude and perspective while experiencing something different.

The value of traveling, aside from pleasure, is when you take your time to explore the ideas, customs, and social behavior of a people. It is vital to determine why the people of a specific region are who they are. Growth comes when you empathetically learn about people, and then you add that knowledge to the tapestry of knowledge gleaned from other experiences. Once you have woven a broad fabric of culture, then you may be able to educate others effectively, and experience growth yourself. Then you will become happier.

Humility Contributes to Happiness

A husband and wife I knew were having financial trouble, and I went over to their house to help them. In the process of helping them, I noticed that their electricity bill was extremely high, and they were paying way too much. I proceeded to show them another electric company that was less expensive. I showed them how to make the transition from the current company to the new one and how much they would save. However, I did not do it for them.

A few months later, I went back to their house and asked them if they had made the change to the new company. They had not. In a couple of months, I asked them again if they had made the change to the new company. They had not. They never did change electric companies, and as a result, they paid about $1000 more that year in electricity costs. What a waste! I don't know if it was a lack of humility, laziness, or both, but it shows the importance of being humble and following through on the helpful advice of ones with experience. Unfortunately, sometime people mistakenly equate humility with weakness.

Humble, Yet Confident! Humility is Not Weakness

My father was a veterinarian. He went into business for

himself when I was a baby, and he had a partner. This partner was a brilliant man; one of those gifted individuals who come along only once in a blue moon. This man was also humble. In spite of his humility, he was confident in his abilities, and there was one particular incident that demonstrated this confidence.

He was one of the first black veterinarians in South New Jersey. When he took the state boards, he scored extremely high. I not sure how high, but probably one of the top scores to date, according to my father. However, his score was so high that the board failed him. How could that be? He had never failed a test in his life. The committee assumed that a black man could not score that high on this test. Undaunted, he went and stood before the Board and stated that he knew this material better than anyone. He then said, *"If you do not believe me, you can give me the test right now!"* Shocked and amazed, the board passed him immediately with no further questions.

Being humble is good, but when you know your stuff, don't be afraid to show it when necessary. Humility is not weakness, and properly displayed, can have financial benefits.

Understand Your Limitations for Your Benefit

For many people, their ego is the biggest obstacle that keeps them from reaching their full financial potential. Justified confidence is reasonable, but overconfidence is detrimental to success. It is essential to know your limitations in life and financially successful people know their limitations.

All of us do not have the same skill set, abilities, or intelligence. When someone is more proficient at something than you, there is no shame in asking them or paying them to help. By being humble in this way, you can benefit financially.

Pharmaceutical entrepreneur Ewing Marion Kauffman said, "If you hire people you consider smarter than you, you are more likely to listen to their thoughts and ideas, and this is the best way to expand on your own capabilities…"

Politician R.H. Grant, once said, "When you hire people that are smarter than you are, you prove you are smarter than they are."

Acknowledging that people are smarter than you are is an indication that you have a firm understanding of your limitations and that you want to be successful in your endeavors. So, if being humble can lead to success, then being humble is directly related to financial happiness.

Avoid Credit Cards – Well, Kind of

After we purchased our first house, it was virtually empty. We had little in the way of furniture or decorations. However, soon after we bought the house, I received a new credit card with a $1200 limit. I laugh at that credit limit now, but back then, it was a lot. With no furniture in the house and a new credit card, I went to my wife and said, "Let's buy stuff for the house and max out the credit card." I literally said, let's spend every bit of that credit. Without a moment's hesitation, my wife said yes, and that's what we did. To this day, I only remember one of the items that we purchased; a cheap print of the Grand Canyon.

What a dumb thing to do. There was no need to fill our house with decorations and non-essential living items. We had a bed and hand-me-down living room furniture given to us by my grandparents. We had a television that sat in the middle of a large family room area filled with little but air. However, we wanted more stuff to help fill the space. The problem was, we didn't have the money to do so, and we charged it!

Soon after that, I was borrowing from Peter to pay Paul. At this point in my life, I would come home from work, eagerly anticipating the mail. Why? I was hoping for a new credit card application that offered balance transfers with no interest for a certain number of months. I can still see the advertisements,

"Transfer balances and pay no interest for twelve months." "No balance transfer fee, and don't pay any interest for six months."

I would eagerly fill out the application, wait for the new card, and then transfer the balance from one of my maxed-out credit cards to the new one. This cycle went on for a couple of years.

Those were rough times because we did not have any breathing room financially. If we had a problem with one of our cars, we had to pay for it with a credit card. It took me many, many years to get out of that cycle of financial torture.

When Credit Cards are Bad

Credit cards are dangerous and make it easy to purchase things you don't need. They also create the thinking that you are not spending real money because a cash transaction doesn't take place. You never "see" the money. Undisciplined use of them makes a person even more unhappy because if you don't pay off your balance before the end of the month, you pay interest and now owe more than the item is worth. You may even find yourself paying for something long after the thing or its usefulness is gone.

When Credit Cards are Good

Credit cards are useful when the user is disciplined. However, many people must learn to be disciplined to use credit cards effectively.

Use credit cards to get points but avoid finance charges by paying off the balance immediately after the purchase. You can use the points earned for many things from airplane tickets, gift cards at restaurants and stores, or even cashback. Know yourself and your weaknesses before using them.

Neither my wife nor I have accumulated interest on a credit card in well over a decade and a half. We have, however, used credit cards extensively during that time. We pay them off before interest is applied. We will then use the points to go out on date nights at various restaurants or to the movies.

The Danger of Debit Cards

Debit cards or check cards, like credit cards, are easy and convenient. They are also more practical than credit cards because they don't allow us to spend more than you have in the bank. Like a check, when we use a debit card, the money is removed directly from our checking account.

When we use debit cards regularly, it is challenging to keep track of what we spend. Many of us cannot keep track of every purchase in our minds. That takes an exceptional person with a great memory, awareness, and discipline.

Debit and credit cards make it easy to spend money on things we don't need even if we have the money in the bank. They are budget busters. For example, it is easy to use a card to buy a five-dollar cup of coffee, potato chips at a convenience store or something else purchased spontaneously. These impulse buys can destroy a budget quickly. So be careful in how you use debit cards.

Smart Thinking When Buying a Home

Our second house was my favorite house of the four we've owned over the years. I loved driving into the subdivision because there was beautiful architectural landscaping as you entered the development, and trees were everywhere. The residents in the neighborhood took care of their yards, and the area was very green. The subdivision also had a relatively low-cost homeowner's association, which help maintain the quality and value of the homes and community.

It's interesting how we found that house. My wife and I were viewing a house that was for sale on the same street. We looked at the home but determined the owners were asking too much for it. That home was on a dead-end road, so we had to drive to the end of the street to turn around and exit the subdivision. As we were driving to the end of the street, we notice a man moving furniture out of a house and asked him what he was doing. He said he was selling his mother's home, but it was not yet on the market. So, we asked him if we could look inside the house because we were in the market for a home. He said yes, and we went inside.

This house had not been updated since it was built in the early 80s. It was very dark but had beautiful dark paneling in the family room, the kind you would see in fancy dens of large mansions. It was a large traditional home with a living room, dining room, and kitchen that were all separate. It was about 3500 square feet with an unfinished basement. However, it did not have an open floor plan and was dark. My wife hated it!

Undeterred, I asked the man how much he was asking for the house, and he said about $30,000 less than the home we had looked at on the same street. This home was bigger and also had a full unfinished basement. The other house did not have a basement. I quietly told my wife that we needed to purchase this house even though it was not the layout we wanted.

After some impressive convincing on my part, she reluctantly said yes. I explained how we could update this home with little money and that we would have instant equity in the house, besides it checked all of the other boxes that were important to us such as an excellent school district, a quiet dead-end street, and was surrounded by well-maintained homes. We bought it, and it proved to be a beautiful house after our updates. Then, the housing crisis hit.

It was the middle of the economic recession, and we were selling our home so we could downsize into a smaller house in a less expensive area. Doing so would cut our home expense in half without extending the loan beyond our current mortgage end date. Also, our children were adults now, and we no longer needed that big house. Additionally, we wanted to decrease our expenses so we could have more money and flexibility to help others and travel.

As we were at the closing table and the bank was cutting us a big check for the money, we made on the house our realtor was amazed. She said, "This is the first time this year that someone I know has made money from the sale of their house." To tell the truth, I was a little surprised myself. However, when purchasing this house, we applied many of the investment principles my father taught me to think about when buying a home. The advice paid off!

What to Do – Think Investment First

The adage of "buy the worst house in the best neighborhood" is still good advice. My father gave me this advice when I was very young, maybe 8 or 9 years old. However, I didn't understand the full importance of the instruction. So, I feel it is necessary to qualify why this is good advice.

Always remember that a house is an investment first, and the average person often builds wealth through their home. When buying a home, that is the first thing you need to keep in mind. Sure, there are certain features and personal wants you may desire in a house, but that should be secondary. By this, I mean, if you have to sacrifice a few desired features for the sake of a good investment, do it. Decide on a home with your head and not your heart.

Don't be scared away from a rundown home for $210,000 in a neighborhood of $300,000 homes. You may immediately want to walk away from this ugly home with weird colors, holes in the walls, a jungle for a yard, urine-stained carpets, and a layout that does not quite fit your wants. However, you may be able to spend, let's say, $40,000 to get that rundown home up to your standards and the neighborhood's standards. If you do this, you instantly have $50,000 of equity in your "new" home. If you wanted to, you could then sell the house and have that money in your pocket.

Essential Things to Keep in Mind When Buying A Home

- Buy homes in the best school districts
- Buy on dead-end streets or cul-de-sacs where there is little traffic
- Depending on where you live, avoid cookie-cutter homes and purchase in established neighborhoods with trees
- Buy houses in up-and-coming areas
- Never buy a great house in a bad neighborhood
- Avoid homes near powerlines, flood zones, or that back up to major roads

Doing these things will increase the number of prospective buyers when you go to sell your home. Even if you never intend to sell, these principles are sound because you will most likely sell the house even though you do not think you will. Remember, change is constant.

What Not to Do – Don't Overspend

When a lender determines how much they will loan, you may hear terms like housing-to-income ratio or debt-to-income ratio. They will use these two ratio-based guidelines to evaluate how much you can borrow. The amount you can borrow will depend on several factors, but make sure that you feel comfortable making your monthly mortgage, tax payments, and insurance along with the bills for all your other monthly expenses, including estimated home maintenance and repairs.

I've purchased three homes in my life, and every time I applied for a loan, the bank said I qualified for a house that was much more expensive than I thought I could afford. When they give you the approval, the tendency is to buy a house that is at the maximum bank-approved amount. For example, when we purchased our second house, my wife and I set a maximum amount that we would spend on the house. Our maximum amount was considerably lower than the bank approved amount. While we were looking at houses, we did not immediately find what we were looking for in our price range, so we kept inching the price higher and higher. We ended up purchasing a house that was higher than our original budget, but still lower than the bank approved amount. This experience does show the role human nature plays in purchasing something like a house.

The danger in using the bank's numbers is that you can become house poor. Being house poor means that after you buy the house, you have a little money to pay for the necessary things to furnish and maintain the home. Being house poor is a dangerous position to be in because when things go wrong with the house, and something will go wrong, you have very little money to fix the problems. Often, the solution is to go into debt to correct the problem.

Conversely, if you buy a home that is well below what the bank says you can afford, then you have the money to pay for unexpected problems, money to put into the bank, and money to enjoy life.

Plan for Additional Homeownership Expenses

Maintaining a home involves several expenses. The exterior of the house, depending on the type of surface, may require staining every few years, painting every 10-15 years, or little maintenance if it is brick. You may have to factor in the significant expense of buying a new roof at some point. It would help if you considered future high-cost purchases like a furnace and air conditioning unit as well as kitchen appliances.

You will have homeowner's insurance in case something catastrophic happens to the house, but have you factored in the cost of the deductible? What about equipment expenses for the maintenance of the yard? The bottom line is, remember to consider all the things you are likely to spend money on when estimating the total monthly cost of homeownership. It is much more than just principle, interest, taxes, and insurance.

Smart Thinking When Buying a Car

Without a doubt, our family has saved more money by buying used cars and only carrying liability insurance than any other cost-cutting measures. My wife and I have purchased three new vehicles during our married life, but once we paid off the last one, which was the last of our debt, we have only bought used cars.

One year I was looking for an older model Lexus because I knew those cars would drive for 250,000 miles effortlessly. I saw a Lexus advertised in the classifieds, and I drove about 30 miles to see it. The car was beautiful and drove perfectly. It had about 120,000 miles on it, and the timing belt was recently changed. Cha-ching! The owner of the car and I then went directly to my bank and finalized the transaction inside the bank. I paid about $3600 cash for the car and drove it another 120,000 miles.

In the area we lived at the time, many wealthy people would sell their cars so that they could buy the newest and latest models. Cars to them were a status symbol. Their old cars were the ones that I would buy. I would pay cash for them because, at this point in my life, I was debt-free, had savings, and didn't want to purchase full-coverage insurance. The money I saved was incredible.

A car should never be looked at as a financial investment

unless you are a collector of antique cars. Suffice to say, most of us are not car collectors. Even high-end vehicles are not investments since you will never be able to sell your car for more than you pay for it.

Working smart to put yourself in a position to pay for a car with cash is extremely beneficial. People typically finance a used car by getting a loan from a bank. Because of interest charges, you are going to pay much more for a financed car than one paid with cash. You will never recoup the money spent on a financed car.

The value of a vehicle is having a car or truck that you can rely on, and that fits the needs of your family without breaking your budget. Owning a car or truck as a status symbol is not financially smart.

Buying Used Cars

When purchasing a used vehicle, look for high-quality models most likely to last 200,000 miles or more. A quick search on the internet will help you find these vehicles.

Used Car vs. New Car – Savings

The chart below shows how much money can be saved over five years when you buy a quality old car instead of a new one. While the monthly maintenance cost of an old car may be considerably higher than a new car, the overall monthly expense and long-term expenditures are drastically lower than owning a new car.

	Used Car	New Car
Initial Cost	$6,000	$28,000 with $5000 down
Monthly Payment	$0	$428.79
Insurance Month	$52 (Liability-Only)	$290 (Full Coverage)
Monthly Maintenance	$150	$44
Cost over 60 months	$18,120	$50,767.40

Find What You Like to Do and Make That Your Career

As I mentioned earlier, my father was a good but demanding man. When he stopped paying for college after my first semester because I had poor grades, I changed my major from Finance to Fine Arts. That may seem like a significant change, but graphic design and fine art were my first love. I graduated from college with a Fine Arts degree and subsequently went into the commercial art and graphic design industry. While my career evolved over the years from graphic design to web development, I never regretted the change.

Many do not like their job, and some even dread going to work each day. However, I have always enjoyed going to work and enjoyed the people with whom I worked. My jobs never seemed like real "jobs" to me because I realized early in my adult life that if you choose a career that you love, you'll never have to "work" a day in your life.

In the middle of my career, I worked for a particular company for about five years. Working for this company was my favorite job because it allowed me to have complete creative freedom. However, the company did not pay much money, so I eventually moved on to another company to increase my salary. In those days, one of the best ways to improve your pay was to change jobs. Jobs were plentiful. Shortly after that, another, more prominent, company hired me, and I worked there for about 14 years. During that time, I transitioned from design work to web development and programming. I also fell in love with web development.

I have been blessed never to need to take a job I hated just because I was desperate for money. I am not sure how I would handle that situation, but I would never discourage nor belittle people who would take any job to survive.

Again, I have never dreaded going to work. So, the adage of, "Choose a job that you love, and you'll never have to work a day in your life" is accurate. Sure, there may be aspects of any job that we may not enjoy, but if 90% of your work involves what you like to do and 10% does not, that still seems like a darn good ratio.

Be Great at Your Job

No matter what you do for work, be in the top 15% of the people who do that job – although I'm not sure how you would measure that. Feel good about your work. Undoubtedly it is less strenuous to be great at your job if you love what you're doing; if you have a passion for what you are doing. It does require that you be a student of your work and disciplined. Take pride in learning to do your job well. Cultivate pride within yourself related to that job. It is vital to develop confidence in one's worth or abilities and to be able to sit back and say, "I did that...That is pretty good."

Oseola McCarty, an African American woman who washed clothes for a living and who gave away a life savings of $150,000 to help strangers get a college education at the University of Southern Mississippi, said this: "There's a lot of talk about self-esteem these days...It seems pretty basic to me. If you want to feel proud of yourself, you've got to do things you can be proud of. Feelings follow actions."

With this in mind, why not let your job be one of the things about which you are proud?

Martin Luther King Jr. eloquently said, "If a man is called to be a street sweeper, he should sweep streets even as a Michelangelo painted, or Beethoven composed music or Shakespeare wrote poetry. He should sweep streets so well that all the hosts of heaven and earth will pause to say, 'Here lived a great street sweeper who did his job well.'"

Proverbs 22:29 states, "Do you see a man skillful at his work? He will stand before kings; He will not stand before common men."

Finding What You Love to Do

Jessica Nabongo, a UN employee turned travel blogger, became the first black woman to visit every country on earth. What I find interesting is that she had a six-figure job at a pharmaceutical company. However, she left the job because it did not satisfy her. She did not love that job, but she did enjoy traveling. She subsequently founded a travel company and went on her world-wide travel quest. She now makes a good living from her passion.

If you are uncertain about what you would like to do as a career, take a Myers-Briggs Type Indicator test. It is a personality test that will, among other things, tell you about yourself and help you assess what jobs or careers you are best suited for based on your personality.

If you are a parent of teenagers who seem to be directionless, have them take the test. I did this with my son, and he chose one of the professions suggested for his personality type. He loves his job and is good at it.

Maintain Balance in Your Life and Work

Work-Life Balance and Perception

In the United States, the average lifespan is about 78 years. The US retirement age is around 67 years of age. That leaves about 11 years of "freedom" to do whatever you want. Unfortunately, it's during a time in life when physically you may not be able to enjoy it. That is why it is it is essential, while you are young and working, to maintain an excellent work-life balance. Enjoy living while you are at the peak of your health and in the prime of your life.

While work is vital and can be a rewarding part of our lives, it can become so all-consuming that we neglect other, equally critical, or more essential features of life. A balance needs to be struck, which effectively balances work obligations with home life and building rewarding relationships with others. Doing this requires awareness, a conscious effort, planning, discipline, and an understanding that a work-centric life is unbalanced.

You find some people who are workaholics in their professional life. Their work comes first in their lives. What is their goal? No doubt some of these people enjoy their careers, and for this small segment of the population, this is a great privilege. However, many people work to maintain a lifestyle.

Working to Maintain a Lifestyle

People love big homes and fancy cars, and they work most of their lives so that they can acquire and keep these things. However, they rarely get the enjoyment out of them that they anticipated. Also, the type of job that they have to maintain these things can be so stressful that it affects their health and consumes most of their time. Isn't it much smarter to have a modest home and car with more money in your savings account, and more time to actually enjoy life?

Remember, a company is only loyal to their profit margin. A company does not owe you anything other than a paycheck, and that paycheck may end at any time. I write this to emphasize the importance of a work-life balance.

Ecclesiastes 4:6 states, "Better is a handful of rest than two handfuls of hard work and chasing after the wind."

Those who do not maintain a balance often deprive themselves of the fruitage of their "hard work" because they do not have the time nor energy to enjoy living. Later in their workaholic life, they determine that their powers were spent chasing after the wind.

Avoid the Perception Trap

Another thing that hinders work-life balance is perception. It is the perception that if we do not have a big house and a fancy car, then we are less distinguished or successful in the eyes of others. We live our life so that we can be looked at "positively" by people who have little importance in or influence over our lives. It is better to have a $20 purse with $400 in it, than a $400 purse with $20 in it.

We may take on a new job because it promises greater prestige and more income. However, it also comes with working late nights as well as weekends, sometimes spending considerably more than a typical 40-hour workweek. Working like this may result in burnout or chronic exhaustion, anxiety, and frustration. That is not balanced, and it is no way to live. Perception is not always reality.

Don't let the materialistic thinking of those around you change your definition of "success" or "happiness."

Things to Consider - Maintain a Good Work-Life Balance

The correct work-life balance will be different from individual to individual. The differences often depend on the individual's priorities and what stage they are at in their life. A healthy balance for an individual when they are young, may not be a healthy balance for the same people when older. Keep these points in mind when considering the following.

- Continually evaluate what is most important to you and make sure it is not "things."
- Work fewer hours. Working less may require an adjustment in lifestyle or reassuring your employer of your commitment to your job.

- Cultivate interests and friendships apart from your work
- Don't let your life be about getting rich or making money
- Determine if your family is happy with your amount of work
- Prioritize your physical health and mental wellbeing
- Travel to nature-oriented places. Doing so will help you focus on life priorities.
- Understand that you don't have to be perfect
- Leave your work at work, even if you love it
- Learn to say no to yourself, work, and others
- Prioritize family time and personal relationships

Signs of Burnout

- Change in appetite or weight
- Change in sleep habits or chronic exhaustion
- Feelings of withdrawal, isolating yourself from others
- Feeling overwhelmed, stressed, self-doubt, frustrated, or powerless
- Frequent headaches
- Loss of motivation
- Lowered immunity

Buy Used - Garage Sales and Thrift Stores Are Good

I have to admit that I've never been a thrift store kind of guy. The idea of wearing someone else's clothes never appealed to me.

However, one day recently, I was in a thrift store with my wife and a friend. While I was walking around, wasting time while waiting for my wife, our friend mentioned the store had neckties for an excellent price.

I had mentioned to her earlier that I was looking for ties, so I walked over to take a look, more as a way to appease her, than anything. I could not believe what I saw. There were about four ties that I just loved, and they were only a couple of dollars each. So, I bought all of them.

While still waiting for my wife, I happened to walk by the electronics section. I noticed HDMI cables that were around one dollar. I could not believe that! One or two dollars for an HDMI cable that would cost a minimum of $15 retail was an incredible deal.

This experience taught me a valuable lesson. Swallow your pride and prejudices and shop at thrift stores. Even if you are uncomfortable wearing the clothes of other people, there are other items you can purchase, which will allow you to save a considerable amount of money.

Garage Sales and Estate Sales

Garage sales and estate sales are also excellent ways to furnish a home with considerably less money than buying new home furnishings. The items at garage sales are often less expensive than estate sales, but both provide good savings. The advantage of an estate sale is that they often have big-ticket items for sale such as beds, appliances, furniture, and the like. Garage sales tend to have things geared toward decorating and other, smaller, household items like lawnmowers, tools, lamps, whatnots, and more. Often, purchasing from these types of sales will allow you to save from 60 to 90% of retail.

Great Deals Over the Years

Here are some of the significant garage sale purchases we made over the years. While we've bought many things at garage sales like name brand clothes for the children at low prices, these are the purchases that stand out.

- Two years' worth of toner cartridge for $20
- 1st edition of a rare book for $2
- Solid gold chain for $0.50
- Solid wood rice bed and mattress for $100
- A $600 software package for $25
- Set of golf clubs for $15

College Education and Financial Thinking

I graduated from a public university in 1989 and the cost of a college degree has increase significantly since then. I know because I have two children in their 20's and many parents my age are paying their kids' way through college. Among us parents, much conversation has come up concerning the cost and true value of higher education. Is it worth the cost? Should I borrow money to pay for a degree? All good parents are concerned about their children's future. We do everything we can to ensure that our children grow up to enjoy a reasonably comfortable and secure life—a happy life. Therefore, we attach great importance to education.

However, at the time of this writing, the average yearly cost for an academic year at a public university was around $22,000. The cost per year more than doubles to an astounding $48,000 for a private university. That's almost $200,000 for the cost of a college degree. Of course, the true cost varies with many factors such as; are you living at home or will you need room and board, are you an in-state student or out-of-state student; and are you supplementing the cost with a scholarship, etc. What I find even more fascinating than the rising cost of higher education is that people are incurring large loans to finance this "education." This is dangerous because students are finding out that after graduation, they do not make enough money to successfully pay-off that debt. Even when money is not borrowed to pay for the degree, the resulting pay from the degree may not justify the high cost of the degree. So, it is extremely important to factor in the cost of loans, subsequent debt after graduation, and resulting pay from the degree earned to assess the financial risk-reward of going to college. There comes a point when the benefits gained from a university education are less than the amount of money or energy invested in that education. People need to be smart and understand the tipping point. Parents and students need to know how much a particular college degree is worth and will they be able to successfully recoup the investment in their education.

Having said that, it amazes me when people spend $200,000 on a basic private university degree that typically results in a slightly above average USA wage. That doesn't make good fiscal sense. Clearly there are less expensive ways to prepare for a financially stable and happy life, without acquiring a degree at that expense.

My son, who is in his twenties, is married, has a stable job, a nice house, and no college debt. Additionally, many of his friends are in the same situation. Why? They didn't go to a university. My son had his schooling paid for by the IBEW (International Brotherhood of Electrical Workers) and he makes a very comfortable living in low-cost-of-living Georgia as an electrician. Frankly, it is his work habits and personal training that are the primary factors to his "success." Now, my daughter went to a local public university on a scholarship and lived at home to keep the cost of the education to a minimum.

In many ways a college degree is just a credential that opens a door to a prestigious career path but is rarely prepares you for that career. In the case of my son, he learned the job by doing it while going to school. He only needed the equivalent of an Associates of Arts degree, for which he didn't have to pay, to move along his career path. He also has the option to continue his education and increase his pay at a faster rate.

I met a man who owns a landscape company. He left his corporate job, which was associated with his university degree, to start this company which had nothing to do with his degree. He ended up making over six-figures, which was more than he was being paid with his "degree job."

The fact of the matter is that a college education is not needed to be a happy, contented, and financially stable person. If a person alters their thinking of "success," a college degree is not necessary for many career paths. The World Book Encyclopedia states that "Education should help people become useful members of society. It should also help them develop an appreciation of their cultural heritage and live more satisfying lives." One does not need a university degree to be a useful member of society and to lead happy and satisfying lives. In fact, USA Today reports that "70% of the workers in the coming decades will not need a four-year college degree, but, rather, an associate degree from a community college or some type of technical certificate."

Success in life involves more than just material prosperity. Again, I am not saying a college or university degree is not needed at all. Certainly, if you want to become a physician, aerospace engineer, corporate lawyer, or attain some other prestigious career, then a degree is necessary. But frankly, a college education is not a commodity every should "own" or must own. There are many other less expensive ways to be financially stable without borrowing money for a college education or even going to college. In fact, if you are disciplined, frugal, honest, and self-motivated you will find yourself earning more than the typical person in your field. A balanced education should consider that more than being rich is needed to make us truly happy.

Try to Be Self-Sufficient

Being self-sufficient does not mean being selfish.

We had an unfinished basement in our second home, and I wanted to finish it. Since I did not want to spend much money, I decided to be the general contractor of the project. However, I had never done anything like this, so I decided to learn. I went to the permit office and asked the gentleman who distributed permits what was needed to be a general contractor for my basement remodel. He was very eager to help and gave me the information and permits I needed to start.

I got quotes for all phases of the project, including framing, drywall and finishing, electricity, heating and air conditioning, tiling, and plumbing. I then hired the workers and was there for all of the inspections throughout the project. The project went smoothly.

I am not sure how much money was saved by taking the initiative and being self-sufficient, but I am sure it was thousands of dollars. This example shows in a small way, the importance of doing things for yourself instead of paying others to do them. You can learn to do it yourself.

I Thessalonians 4:11 states, "Make it your aim to live quietly and to mind your own business and to work with your hands, so that you may walk decently in the eyes of people outside and not need anything."

Ways to be More Self Sufficient

According to the Merriam-Webster online dictionary, self-sufficiency is the ability to maintain oneself or itself without outside aid. It is the capability of providing for one's own needs. Being self-sufficient may mean learning new skills so you can do things for which you would otherwise need to pay. Here are some ways you can be self-sufficient and benefit yourself as a result:

- Read home improvement books. When something in your house needs repair, learn to do it yourself (DIY).
- Learn to cook from scratch.
- Live simple. The fewer things you have, the fewer things you have to maintain.
- Work for yourself
- Cultivate a garden and grow food
- Learn to sew

The Effects of Patience and Understanding on Happiness

Overall happiness is directly related to the way we think and how we perceive the world. Some people inherently have an optimistic view of the world while others may be a bit more distrustful. Nonetheless, the following story helps us to appreciate the need to incorporate patience and understanding as a core part of our personality. While doing so may or may not help our financial wellness, it will contribute to one's overall happiness.

For almost three years, my wife and I lived abroad in Portugal. This time of temporary immigration led to meeting people of many different cultures and provided delightful experiences. There was one particular learning encounter that teaches all of us a beautiful lesson.

I went into a café, in the town in which I lived, to buy an ice cream bar. A family of Ukrainians owned the café, and the entire family was in the restaurant. We began an enjoyable conversation in Portuguese, and the wife eventually asked me where I was from. Matter-of-factly I told them I am American. However, she asked again, "Where are you from?" I said, "I am from the United States," thinking I didn't say the previous phrase correctly in Portuguese. Nevertheless, her husband asked again, "What nationality are you?" I said, no doubt with a quizzical look on my face, "I'm American. I'm from Atlanta in the United States." "No, no, no, where are your mother and father from Angola, Mozambique, Cape Verde?" I thought to myself, "New Jersey...Philadelphia?" I suddenly realized, in my ignorance, that these Ukrainians were utterly unfamiliar with African American history. So, I patiently explained to them, to the best of my ability and in my limited Portuguese, that as a result of slavery, most blacks in America have lost their history. We typically do not know from which African country we originated. This concept was news to them; probably because they've had limited exposure to black Americans. They were quiet for a moment after the explanation, and then we continued talking, with the wife showing an unexpected sympathy. They were very, very lovely people and after a long and awkward conversation, because of the language barrier, they invited me back to their cafe for dinner.

I have to preface what I learned next with the fact that traveling is my passion, and I love to experience the travels of others, so I am a member of a few online travel groups.

I decided to post this experience on a Facebook travel page for African Americans since this story was directly related to the black American travel experience. I was surprised to learn that many black Americans have had similar experiences while traveling internationally and experiencing other cultures. Surprisingly, even some blacks from African countries had a hard time understanding why black Americans did not know their roots.

In reading the Facebook comments, I was also glad to see that some black Americans understand why there is a disconnect with other nationalities concerning African American history. However, many blacks could not comprehend the divide. So, for those who did not understand, I asked them to think about it this way.

What do you know about the Kurdish diaspora? Do you know the origins of the caste system in India? What happened to the original Tasmanians? Do you know about the violent historical relationship between China and Tibet? What did Afghanistan look like 50 years ago, and what does it look like now, and why? Tell me about the Hungarian or Indochinese diaspora? How much do you know about the history and plight of other nationalities, creeds, and races?

I think my point was clear. Most of us know about the history that shaped our families or us. That's normal and expected. However, even that knowledge is limited for most Americans since we only receive a tainted USA education about history. Frankly, a limited historical perspective is increasingly common among most nationalities. Why is this the norm? In my experience, it seems that many people today are just trying to survive. History is lost on them because they are dealing with their present-day difficulties in life.

I wrote all of this to say, patience and empathy go a long way and directly contribute to happiness. Be patient with ones who do not know and educate when we encounter, but only after we've taught ourselves.

Another thing I found fascinating in this learning experience is that there was a tiny group of people who immediately played the race card after reading this experience. They stated that the Ukrainians were racist. Now, I know the face of racism and prejudice, and this was not it. However, their response shows how some people can only see this world through race-colored glasses. This type of reaction is not specific to one race; a segment in many cultures respond similarly. These few people were superimposing their experiences or cloudy vision on a situation of which they had no knowledge. What do we learn from this?

If we take the time to gain a complete and accurate assessment of a situation before reacting to it, we will likely be more understanding, sympathetic, and patient toward others. So, do not be quick to attribute evil motives. Misreading motives can be one of the fastest ways to stifle communication, education, and potential relationships. Too many times, people miss opportunities for growth and advancement by taking offense when then intent was never to offend. Remember, we are always ambassadors of our particular culture, nationality, creed, or religion. Thus, initially, it is usually best to assume that others want to do what is right rather than attribute wrong motives when situations arise that seem curious. Optimistic and "glass half-full" people are generally happier than their counterparts.

Additionally, educate yourself beyond your own culture and

history. Doing this may enable you to have the perspective to empathize with or effectively educate others by understanding the lenses through which they see the world.

If you perceived that a person's goal was to offend, calmly and patiently explain what hurt you and why it made you feel that way. Understand that sometimes it is our mistaken conclusions that cause us to lose patience. So, don't get upset, make dogmatic statements, or ascribe wrong motives. Inform and educate with a smile. Be patient, understanding, and don't be quick to take offense.

Following these principles will contribute to your happiness.

Parents, Teach Your Children to Work & More

I was having a conversation with one of my neighbors, and I told her what my son was doing to earn money. He was cutting grass and doing odd jobs for those in the neighborhood. However, my neighbor said, "Oh, my son would never do that." She said it almost condescendingly as if manual labor was a bad thing. What she didn't understand were the principles and values you learn from doing hard work at a young age.

When I was a child, my father would never give me money unless I worked for it. I remember one time I wanted five dollars to go to a carnival. He said he would give me the money, but I had to weed the flower bed after I got back. That was the one job I hated the most as a child, weeding. However, I wanted to go to the fair. He gave me the money, and when I got home, as much as it pained me, I weeded the flower bed. My childhood is full of experiences like this. I cannot remember one time my father gave me money without me having to work for it.

My dad was not a brilliant individual, but he was smart. He was also the hardest worker I've ever seen in my life. People think that the harder you work to make a living, the less successful you are. That is not true. My father achieved a measure of success in his career, mostly through hard work. He tried to instill those values and me. I think he succeeded.

When it came time for me to buckle down and get out of my severe financial debt, it was not difficult. I was used to hard work and discipline. The foundation that my father gave me made it more manageable during those times.

Teach your children to be industrious. Assist them in taking a real interest in hard work. It doesn't matter if the job seems menial, or it is not the type of work you want them to choose as a career, endeavor to have them become skillful at the task. Hard work leads to a sense of accomplishment and self-worth. Developing this level of industriousness will have monumental life and financial benefits for them in the future.

Children Need Direction

Children without direction from a parent or mentor are at a clear disadvantage in this world. I know a person who is very smart, disciplined, and studious. However, they chose a career that was low-paying because, as a youth, they did not have sufficient parental direction related to education. You have probably met these people. They are smart, yet they are doing things that do not equal their talents or gifts. If they love their job, that's fine, but often they do not and are floundering in their secular career.

Other Things to Teach Your Child

- Teach self-control
- Teach your child about consequences
- Teach delayed gratification

- Teach them to complete unpleasant tasks
- Teach them to put others before themselves
- Teach your child to prioritize
- Teach your child to be an example

All of the things above, when learned, will have a beneficial financial impact on the child's life. They will also contribute to the child's overall happiness.

Strategic Thinking and Happy Decisions

A Personal Story

When I was in elementary school, a much older cousin taught me how to play chess. I was captivated by the game but did not understand how the game would help shape my life and thinking.

I joined a chess club in middle school and had a teacher who helped foster my love for the game. I even got to the point where I became the chess champion of my middle school.

During my youth, I had the mind to remember multiple moves in advance and variations off of those moves. It was then that I began to relate that thinking to scenarios in life. I was able to apply the principles I learned by playing this game to circumstances that would come up in my life. I was able to anticipate problems and have a plan of action if they occurred. It prevented those problems from being worse than they needed to be.

Life can change quickly, and the unexpected can happen at any time. So, it is essential to be nimble in our thinking. In life, we need to be able to anticipate the unexpected, know what to do when it occurs, and then respond practically. That is the game of chess in a nutshell. When you apply that way of thinking to your life, you will be less likely to be caught unaware. As a result, you have fewer problems. Fewer problems lead to greater happiness.

Chess and Thinking Agility

Learn chess. That may seem strange. Why learn to play chess? Because chess teaches you a way of thinking that is valuable in life. Chess teaches you to think of various scenarios and deviations from those scenarios. It helps you to minimize mistakes in life and as a result, maximize financial benefits. Chess teaches you to reason that if something out of your control goes wrong, you should have a backup plan. You must always assume that something will eventually go wrong, and you must plan for that scenario.

Chess teaches the importance of planning far in advance, assessing and predicting, strategizing, coming up with alternatives, not being self-centered, reacting to disappointment, re-running scenarios, mutual agreement, concentration, consequences of lapse of thought, foresight, verbal and nonverbal communication, critical thinking, and more.

If you are a parent of young children, encourage or teach them chess at an early age. It is much more than a game. The principles of thinking learned in this game apply to all aspects of life.

Take a Chance

The entrepreneurial spirit was always a part of me, maybe because my father was a business owner. When I was a teenager, I would rent tables at comic book conventions to sell my comics. After graduating from college, I immediately started a graphic design business. I loved the control of doing things the way I wanted them done and to see things grow.

Many years later, I was working for a good company, and by this time in my life, things were great financially. We were out of debt and had savings. While with this company, I learned web development and programming. So, to further my knowledge, I decided to build a website.

I looked at a popular niche website on the Internet and thought to myself, "I can build a better community than that." Then I found out the website was making good money. I told my wife that I was going to build a site and that I thought we could make a little money from it. Maybe it would help us pay for a night out every once in a while, or even a vacation once a year.

She said skeptically, "How can you make money from that?" She was so skeptical that she dismissed the idea and went on her way. Frankly, I didn't know how it would work out, but I was willing to take the chance. There was minimal risk involved because I had a job, and I didn't need to invest much money to build and maintain this website.

I built the website over time, and we were so excited the first time I made a dollar in one day. My wife was shocked. At the end of the month, we spent that unexpected money on dinner, although it did not pay for the entire dinner.

Because I was working a job that I loved, I did not devote much time to this website; however, in a couple of years, it was making $100 a month, then $200. We decided to start using this extra money for vacations. A little while longer, it was making more money: $400 a month, $800 a month, $1200 a month. Within about seven years, we were making enough money to almost live off the passive income from a website that was not even the focus of my energies. I was still working a regular job. I often wonder how much faster the site could have grown if it were my focus. Nevertheless, the site would eventually allow me to stop working and start a web development business.

Imagine if I had never taken the chance to build it. Imagine if I had agreed with my wife that it would never make money. The moral of the story is clear. Go out on the limb, take a chance, be patient, and don't listen to people who doubt you. If you have an entrepreneurial spirit, fulfill that desire.

Think Long Term

The fourth-year after I started the website mentioned earlier, I was thinking about selling it. I had made $3000 that year, and someone wanted to pay me $14,000 for the site. I was very close to selling it, but something inside told me not to sell it. I thought of the long-term potential of the website, and there was no reason for me to sell it other than the instant gratification of that extra money. I am so glad I did not sell. Within another three years, the website was, in one year, making four times the $14,000. Whew, that was close!

Thinking long-term is one of the hardest things for people to do because we live in a society of instant gratification. Society tells us that we deserve the best, and we deserve it right now. As a result, people want to immediately come out of college and be at the top of their profession. Others will change careers and want to make the same amount of money as a person who has been in that career for ten years.

When it comes to financial investments, always think about the long-term potential of that investment. When it comes to non-financial decisions, think about the long-term ramifications of that decision first. Doing so will contribute to your current and long-term happiness.

Other Advice for Happy Financial Living

Don't Waste Time (TV, Video Games, and More)

Wasting time means spending time on things that are either unproductive or that take time away from productive things. For example, spending time surfing the internet or social network sites, playing video games, watching TV, and doing similar things with no goal in mind is a waste of time and creative brainpower.

These things can be a pleasant and relaxing diversion, but when they interfere with more productive things like learning, becoming better at your job, spending time with family or friends, or devoting time to a hobby that has long-term benefits, they become a problem. They can damage motivation and the establishment of family and financial priorities.

Ways to Be More Efficient and Effective

- Designate certain days as time-wasting free days
- Make a daily to-do-list
- Schedule the most important things first
- Set goals related to productive activities
- Keep a log of how much time you spend doing activities
- Do high priority things when you have the most energy

While my wife and I were raising our children, there were times when we would get rid of cable television. We would go without cable for six months or so. During that time, we would do more things together as a family, and we spent more time doing other productive things. It paid off in drawing our family closer together.

Understand the Purpose of Life Insurance

Don't look at life insurance as an investment. Look at it as a way to protect your loved ones in case the breadwinner of the family dies, and the family's savings do not allow the family to be self-insured.

Stick to term life insurance, which is the most basic type of insurance. It covers your family for a specified period (term). If you die within that term, your family receives the amount insured.

There are better types of investments than permanent forms of life insurance, such as whole life insurance, universal life insurance, and variable life insurance. While these types of life insurance promote some kind of long-term cash value, you should invest your money elsewhere.

Continue Learning and Honing Your Skills

I worked for a Fortune 500 company as a user interface designer/web developer for about 14 years. The company encouraged its employees to continue honing their craft through learning. Employees were required to take continuing education classes every year.

It was during this time that I migrated from a user interface designer to web development because of the needs of the company. I then began to use those newly learned skills to create an exit strategy to leave the company because I knew that corporations have little loyalty for a person my age and salary. I was correct. After 14 years with the same company, I was laid off.

Nevertheless, because of my desire to continue learning, I went from knowing nothing about programming and development to owning my own small web development company, which supported our family for many years after the layoff. How glad I am that I didn't take continuing education lightly.

Don't Make Excuses

You are accountable. My father was a no excuse, reap what you sow kind of man. My college experiences related earlier in the book were a testament to that. When my father said he was no longer paying for college after my first semester of bad grades, there was no one to blame but myself.

I could've made excuses as to why I got terrible grades, but there was no excuse other than I was having too much fun and neglecting my schoolwork. I could have dropped out of college, but for me, that would have been a completely unacceptable response to my predicament. I understood that I made poor decisions, and knew it was time to buckle down, be disciplined, study, and pay for the remaining 4 1/2 years of college.

Assume Bad Things Will Happen

Life is not all about flowers, fun, and good times. Soon or later, bad things happen that can affect our happiness and finances. According to debt.org, "...Since 2005, commonly reported causes of bankruptcy include reduced income, job loss, credit debt, illness/injury, unexpected expenses, and preparing for divorce."

Most of the things on this list are beyond our control. That means we should assume bad things are going to happen and plan for them as best we can.

One thing in life is for certain, bad things will happen, and they always seem to occur at the most inopportune times.

We were in the midst of our financial turmoil, but we were making progress and paying off our bills. If we could get through six months or so without anything terrible happening, it would have been great. That did not occur. The transmission on our newest vehicle died, and it cost a considerable amount of money to repair. We did not have the money, so we had to put that $1000 cost onto our credit card. During that time, we were already struggling to pay our bills.

If we had not put ourselves in that bad financial situation to start, this problem would not have been much of an issue.

However, we were struggling to meet monthly expenses as it was, and this happened at one of the worst times possible.

It taught me a valuable lesson. The lesson was, I do not ever want to be in a situation like this again. I do not want to be in a position where if something bad happens, it puts us in an even worse financial predicament.

Other Ways to Save Big Time – What to Avoid

- Lavish Weddings
- Extended Warranties
- Time Shares
- Prestigious Universities
- A Big House

The Secret to Financial Happiness and Happy Living

Live within your means. Live and experience things instead of filling up your life with material possessions. Learn from your mistakes and plan financially so as to minimize the bad times.

The secret to financial happiness is not how much money you make or have, but how smart you are with the money you have. Similarly, happiness is not dependent upon money but how we look at the world and how we live.

Daddy - A Prose Tribute to My Father

Daddy. It's been nine years, nine years, since that 4:00 AM call, and I look at my home (he loved houses) and think... Daddy. Every day, for about a year after the massive stroke shut him down, I would drive home from work, crying like a baby. One year! He was such a monumental figure within our family, as fathers should be. How could one man have been so fallible, and yet influential, governing, respected, grand, and my daddy? I still cry just thinking about him and how I wish he could see my kids again, or my new basement (he loved houses), or even me.

Daddy. He loved to fish. I hated it. However, when I was young, I would ask to go deep-sea fishing with him even though I knew I would get so sick that my bait would never touch the water. I can remember lying in the cabin of the boat, squinting through my thin eyes, as my dad cleaned up my "love" from the cabin floor. I must have spoiled his fishing trip, yet he never said a word - ever (I still can't eat Chuckles to this day). I wasn't sure he even knew why I wanted to go fishing with him. However, when I was nearly 30 years old, I heard him relate to a friend how I hated deep-sea fishing, and I would go just to be with him. He knew (I get seasick to this day)!

Daddy. He grew up in a time when people hated him merely because of the color of his skin. He could not care less what ignorant people thought about him. *He* was going to be helpful and considerate and friendly to you in spite of you and to you. He was kind, selfless, and welcoming because that's who he was. Moreover, he was going to be what he wanted to be and became what he wanted to become, a veterinarian.

Daddy. He was a disciplinarian. I got beatings (not the abusive kind, at least in those days). I was punished. I wasn't free. I was fearful at times (but in the right way). I was loved. I loved him. I knew I was loved even though he never once said it (he would shake my hand with the best of them). In 31 years, he never hugged me. I loved him. Don't miss the point. I embrace and kiss my children; however, sometimes, too much is made of this tangible validation as the only form of love. You know love when you receive it, and there is no doubt in your mind. It is unquestionable and can manifest itself in many other ways…as it did with Daddy…and when you miss that love, you understand, and you may cry, and you may call for Daddy.

www.ingramcontent.com/pod-product-compliance
Lightning Source LLC
Chambersburg PA
CBHW070249220526
45465CB00004B/1564